Gravedigger's Daughter

Vignettes from a Small Kansas Town

Gravedigger's Daughter

Vignettes from a Small Kansas Town

Cheryl Unruh

Meadowlark
PRESS
Emporia, Kansas, USA

Meadowlark Press, LLC
meadowlark-books.com
P.O. Box 333, Emporia, KS 66801

Gravedigger's Daughter
Copyright © Cheryl Unruh, 2021
cherylunruh.com

Cover Image and Design: Dave Leiker
Back Cover Image: Dave Leiker
Interior Images: Looking Up, Anita Byers; A Gust of Wind, Elgie
    Unruh; Letting Time Be, Dave Leiker
Interior Design: Leon Unruh

POETRY / Subjects & Themes/ Family
LITERARY COLLECTIONS/ Essays
BIO&AUTOBIO/ Personal Memoirs

Library of Congress Control Number: 2021948065

ISBN: 978-1-7362232-9-1

"I'm part of the olden days."
Elgie Unruh

For my late father,
Elgie Unruh

Also by Cheryl Unruh

*Flyover People: Life on the Ground
in a Rectangular State*
Quincy Press, 2010

Waiting on the Sky: More Flyover People Essays
Quincy Press, 2014

Walking on Water
Meadowlark Books, 2017

Contents

Gust of Wind

Letting Time Be

Introduction

This collection of vignettes is a memoir about my dad, about me, and about our hometown.

My father, Elgie Unruh, was an interesting character, an eccentric of sorts, and I've long wanted to tell his story, or at least his story as seen through my eyes.

My dad was a caretaker for the Pawnee Rock Township cemetery where he dug and filled graves by hand. He was a carpenter—a craftsman. He drove a school bus and later served as a rural mail carrier. He also created outsider art.

He was born with ichthyosis, a scaly skin condition that affected nearly every aspect of his life. This made him different from other fathers.

I love my mother and my brother, but this book focuses on my dad and me. My parents were separate people who had their own individual lives, and they both loved Leon and me unconditionally.

I was a child of the '60s and '70s. I spent the first 18 years of my life in the house my father built in Pawnee Rock which is a small town in Barton County, in the center of Kansas. In 1960, Pawnee Rock had a population of 380, which grew to 442 people by 1970. The high school closed in 1972, a gut punch for the community. The population has drastically diminished since then.

Pawnee Rock rests in the Arkansas River Valley; the river runs a couple of miles south of town. The town's claim to fame is Pawnee Rock State Historical Site. This outcropping of Dakota sandstone just north of town was a lookout for Native Americans and later for travelers along the Santa Fe Trail.

That's where our story takes place. Now, let me tell you about my father . . .

Cheryl Unruh

Emporia, Kansas

P.S. Memory can be incomplete, flawed, and reinterpreted over time. Any or all of these factors may apply in this memoir.

LOOKING UP

Elgie, Leon, and Cheryl Unruh.

Many Times Over

My dad got kicked out
of high school glee club because,
he said, he wasn't
the right kind of person.

He said he really wanted
to do athletics but couldn't.
He'd play baseball at recess,
but got hot and red in the face
because his skin
was thick and scaly and he
couldn't sweat properly.

He always had
to get at the end of the line
at the drinking fountain.
Sometimes the janitor
wouldn't let him drink
from the fountain at all,
suggesting there was a risk
that my dad's (congenital)
skin disease could infect other kids.

"I had to wait
until class got started
and then ask the teacher
to go out for a drink," he told me.

"I didn't even want to go to school.

"I could've been dead
many times over,
a hundred times over.

"Your grandpa and I would work
with a team of horses
a mile away north
and I'd have to walk home
in the summer heat.
I'd walk home and lay down
in the shade of the sunflowers
in the draw,
in the coolness
where the water had run."

Folded Socks

Sunday morning,
getting ready for church,
I couldn't operate socks yet.
"Sit down here," my dad said
and I climbed onto the couch.
Kneeling in his suit,
Dad stretched thin white socks
over my feet.

The socks were new
and a size too big.
I watched the careful way
he folded the excess cloth
under my toes
and held it in place
as he slipped black Mary Janes
onto my feet.

The bulkiness
of the extra cloth
trapped under my toes
stayed with me
the entire morning,
but the tenderness
of that moment,
the gentleness of my father,
kneeling, helping me
get dressed, well,
I've carried that moment
with me
my entire life.

Learning about Shadows

A 4-year-old learns that shadows
grow with dusk, and that the blackness
of night follows the twilight—
but she's far too young to understand
the shadows and the darkness
humans carry within themselves.

Some evenings when Dad
didn't come home, my mother
loaded my brother and me into the car
and we went to "look for Dad."

He wasn't hard to find. He was
either brooding in his pickup
at the cemetery, or brooding in his pickup
at the Rock where he took down
flags each evening, part of his duties
with the Lions Club.

A kid feels the tension,
wonders if this is the end
of life as she knows it.

Mom stood by the window
of Dad's truck
for a hushed conversation
then returned to the car
saying, "Your dad will be home soon."

The house expanded
with heavy silences,
a cold war between
parents who didn't much
like each other.
A kid doesn't know how
to negotiate that,
afraid she'll be the one
to set off the bomb.

The House My Dad Built

My parents brought me home
from the hospital to a basement house.
An above-ground door led
to 13 wooden stairs, which led
to lime-green walls in the underground
living room and kitchen.
Open concept—one square room.
I shared a bedroom
off the living room
with my older brother.
In our toddler years,
Leon and I wore
matching cowboy pajamas:
cowboys on horses,
lassos hanging in the air.

Meanwhile, my dad
built the house upstairs,
a small rectangular ranch—
kitchen window looking out
over the backyard,
a large picture window
in the living room
facing the street,
two bedrooms on the east side,
a bathroom in the hallway.

About the time I started
to walk, we moved upstairs.
The house had linoleum floors,

a kitchen with aqua Formica.
We sat on furniture Dad made—
a brown, durable couch
with wooden arms,
dining chairs huddled
around the kitchen table for four.

A built-in countertop
stretched the length
of the living room.
Under the wood-grain colored
Formica countertop,
a record player was tucked away
behind sliding wooden doors,
and the record player's
speakers hidden behind
a stretched, green cloth frame.
To decorate the speaker,
my dad soldered a metal staff
with tiny notes rising.

My dad was hard-wired
German practicality,
with a heavy dose
of Mennonite frugality,
but those musical notes
on the staff were just a hint
of the artist
hidden within the man.

Graffiti Kid

I was 3 when I picked up
a green crayon
and scrawled my name
on the bathroom door.

A short time later,
my parents led me to the hallway,
the three of us
facing the now-named door.

Without a word said,
I burst into tears,
becoming aware
in that very moment
that you do not write
your name on doors.

Envy

At 3:30 on a spring afternoon,
standing in turquoise pedal pushers
and my red Keds on the front porch,
hand on the black metal trellis
with white clematis in bloom,
my eyes were peeled to the west,
eager for the first sighting
of my big brother walking his way home
from first grade, books to read in his hand.

Leon got to do things first.
He could run faster, hit the ball farther,
and he knew everything in the world
that there was to know.

Riding the Route

Winter mornings,
    the sky still night,
I rode with my father
to the long white
metal bus barn.

I was too young to be in school,
so on days my mother worked,
I was my father's charge.

A heater warmed the little office
where my dad
and the three other bus drivers
drank Thermos coffee
while the buses idled.
I sat on a wooden chair, unable to touch
the concrete floor, swinging my legs,
listening to the men's morning voices
talk rainfall amounts
or who was leasing whose land.

On the bus, I studied the big kids,
how they laughed together,
teased each other, told stories.
I noticed how the quiet ones
looked out their window
or read books.

As we dropped kids off at
quarter-mile-long driveways,
I memorized who lived where,
learned who the siblings were:
Gary, Craig, Karen.

Riding the sand hills
I stared out the window
to the rolling pastures,
the barbed-wire fences,
the plowed earth.
Trees and barns and farmhouses
became landmarks for me—
the curve in the road I learned
was Darcy's Corner.

Perhaps bouncing
over washboard roads
on those green vinyl seats,
watching the sunrise compete
with the yellow hood of Bus No. 4
is how and when and where
I first came to love our Kansas landscape,
watching darkness open to light,
yawning fields awakening
under a creamy blue sky.

School Bus Driver

Above my dad's head,
above the bus's sun visor
was an angled mirror
which allowed my dad to see
what was going on behind
him as he drove.

When the volume of chatter
increased, when there was
a shout or movement,
someone changing seats,
the bus kids checked that mirror
to see if he saw.

He did.

The mirror reflected his
pale blue eyes, which raised
to the shout,
to the movement.

He knew
that they knew
that he knew.

Not Really a Corn Husker

My father shaved at the sink
in the basement. On the shelf
next to Dad's shaving mirror
sat a bottle of Corn Huskers Lotion,
an opaque, viscous liquid.
Once, as a kid, I tried it myself.
It was slimy and sticky and smelled
something like almond flavoring.

My dad used Corn Huskers Lotion
to moisten his hands and face.
He was born with a form of ichthyosis
and the skin on his arms, legs,
and back was thick and scaly.

This condition
made it difficult for my dad
to sweat properly; he had
to be careful in the summer heat.

But he never complained
about this or about
any circumstance in his life.
He took what he was given
and made the best of it.

Drake & Blackwell

Before he opened
his carpentry shop,
my dad built wooden truck beds
for Drake and Blackwell,
D & B Truck Beds,
a business in downtown
Pawnee Rock.

"My first car
was a 1929 Model A,"
Dad told me.
"I bought it in 1945 with money
I earned from Drake and Blackwell.
I paid $200 cash. I had saved
$20 each week for it."

He had tried to join
the Army, fight
in World War II,
but with his skin condition
he failed his physical exam,
so he built truck beds instead.

Elgie's Craft Shop

In 1948, Dad started his own business,
Elgie's Craft Shop,
on the east side of Centre Street
in a red brick building
with a covered driveway.
Once upon a time
the structure had housed
a garage and service station.

Natural light flowed in
through large plate-glass windows
looking west toward the grocery store
and north toward his driveway
and the lumberyard beyond.
Farmers Elevator was behind him,
the post office kitty-cornered
on this, the main intersection
of Pawnee Rock.

Using three table saws
and a long workbench,
my dad built cabinets and bookshelves.
He upholstered and welded.
He painted houses and served
as a handyman.

For heat, Dad fed wood scraps
into his cast-iron potbelly stove.
When he opened the stove's door,
I'd become entranced

with the dancing fire inside the dark cavern,
its energy hungry and wild.

I was Dad's faithful sweeper of sawdust,
pushing the wide broom on the smooth
concrete floor, then using the hand brush to
pull white wooden curls into a dust bin.

Using scrap lumber and plastic packaging
from drawer pulls, I nailed together
an imaginary weather station
which supposedly measured temperature,
rainfall, and wind speed.

And I sat on the concrete floor and began
my study of the states of the Union
and the counties of Kansas.
Above the plate-glass window on the west
was a colorful array of license plates
from every state in the country.
Above the plate-glass window on the north,
105 license tags, one from every county
in Kansas, all from 1965, white lettering
on a red background.

"Dad. What's RS county?"
"Russell."
"Dad. What's NO county?"
"Neosho."

I can only imagine that
my dad's productivity
was greatly diminished
with me around.

The Pee Pan

There was no restroom
at my dad's shop.
Our house was only
a block-and-a-half away,
but my dad had his own solution
for me: a pee pan.

In his office area, out of view
of the main room, my dad
kept a pee pan tucked away,
an old kitchen saucepan
with a handle.

When the need arose, Dad
got the pan out for me
and gave me privacy.

Then Dad carried the pan
to the ditch and poured it out.
No one was the wiser;
the ditch, after all, was where
he cleaned his brushes.

Betty's Cafe

When I was 4 and hanging
   out with my dad in his shop,
I'm sure I danced in a little circle
on days he told me
that we'd take an afternoon break
at Betty's.

Betty's Cafe was across the street
and just down the block a bit—
a building painted Pepto-Bismol pink,
under a neon sign on a rusted pole outside
advertising Schlitz beer.

Dad and I sat on swivel stools at the bar,
away from the old men
who spent most of their afternoons here
drinking beer. Betty manned
the grill behind the counter,
making a hamburger for one of them.

I studied Betty, this woman
with black, slicked-back hair,
white button-down shirts,
men's trousers and shoes.
Nobody questioned her attire,
no one else seemed to notice,
so I, too, figured that's
just the way she dressed.

Dad ordered two bottles of Pepsi
and pulled a bag of peanuts
from a rack on the counter.
He opened the bag and poured
them into his bottle, saving a few
peanuts for me to drop into mine.

Sunday Nights

On Sunday nights my dad,
brother, and I climbed into Dad's
'48 Chevy pickup and rode three miles
to Grandma's farm and the two-story farmhouse
where Dad spent his childhood.

Grandma sometimes had questions
about bills or oil leases and Dad helped her
with that. She asked Leon and me about school.
Dad ate a piece or two of that awful ribbon candy
that was always leftover from Christmas.

Leon and I sat at the table,
or in Grandpa's empty chair, and read
the weekly *Grit* newspaper, or whatever else
was sitting on the dining room table
and was readable.

Grandma owned a console TV—
with a remote control even—
but she had little use for a TV
or for any newfangled machine
that she had been talked into buying.

Beyond our conversations,
the house spoke—it would creak in the wind,
the clock would chime on the quarter hour
or maybe the phone would ring,
a call for someone else on the party line.

When it was time to go, Grandma handed Dad
a dozen eggs and a cherry pie. "Now if the pie's
not sweet enough, lift up the top crust
and sprinkle on more sugar," she said each week.

Grandma held open the old wooden door
for us and as she said goodbye,
loneliness settled into her voice
as she steeled herself
for another stretch of silence.

Looking Up

The mound of dirt on the sheet of plywood
rose as my dad cut through
the earth with his shovel, flinging
loose dirt out of the rectangular hole.

Taking a break from digging,
he lifted himself
out of the grave.

"Can I go in now?" I asked.
Dad held me by my raised arms and
lowered me. He was about
four feet down in the digging and
I was deep inside the belly of the earth.

I laid my body down on the bottom
of the grave, the coolness of dirt
seeping through my scalp,
my shirt, the back of my bare legs.

I looked up at the summer sky,
a faded blue, evergreen trees framing
my view, and I wondered what it would
be like to be dead, to be lying
deep in the ground. Would I be
waiting for something more to happen
or would I be content if this was it?

Preparations

Early May was the "getting ready
to be ready" time for cemetery grooming
at the Pawnee Rock Township Cemetery
on top of the hill just north of town.

Spring rains grew the runaway grass
and you had to keep up with it in case
the skies rained for a week and you
didn't get another chance to mow.

As soon as my brother and I grew
our hands big enough to hold clippers,
we were up there, trimming grass
around the stones with our mom
while Dad's mower kept a steady roar
in the background.

When my hand and forearm muscles
ached from clipping, I'd climb a juniper
that had a good sitting place,
my back against the trunk.
I'd peel strips of the loose bark
to get to the red and yellow swirls
beneath and watch ants dart out
from their hiding places.

Your work is judged
not by how much is done,
but by what is left undone,

so everything had to be trimmed again
on the last day before the cars began
crawling on the sand-and-sticker roads
so the family members left behind
could place their Memorial Day peonies,
a bouquet in a Folgers Coffee can,
weighted against the Kansas wind
with a few inches of sand and water.

The Undoing

The water was the worst part.
It was smelly and leaned toward green.
We dumped the slimy liquid
onto the cemetery's sand road
and tossed the wilted flowers
into the bed of Dad's pickup.

A week or so after Memorial Day,
my family spent a morning
combing the cemetery,
removing dead flowers,
and placing the plastic flowers
closer to the headstones.

Vases that had value were set
close to the cab of the truck
and everything else
was in a heap in the bed—
the peonies, their petals splayed,
the makeshift vases
of red Folgers cans
and Hellman's Mayonnaise jars.

We started at the south end,
the older end of the cemetery
where people had been buried
long ago. There weren't many
flowers there. As we cleared a section
Dad would move his truck forward,
then around the corner and we
headed back south.

It was a dirty job
and by June that morning sun
turned on you, became less of a friend.
Still, there was something satisfying
about doing manual labor.
You could look out around you,
see what you'd done,
see your day's work,
know you had made the world
a tiny bit better.

Dad, on Digging Graves

"It took Virgil and I two hours
to get through the frost line,"
Dad told me about
one wintertime grave.

"The graves had to be
straight down. They were
pretty particular about that.

"I could go up to the cemetery
and point out every grave I dug
in those 18 or 20 years.

"The last five years
was machine dug.
I could've had it earlier
but I didn't want the marks
the machine left on the ground.
It interfered with mowing."

A Secret Garden

Our house sat on a double lot,
the backyard a jungle
of shrubs and perennials.

Against the east fence
were three lilacs under which
I tucked myself
and read Nancy Drew mysteries.
A bit north of the lilacs
a stand of bamboo produced
javelins and swords for play.

We had fruit trees—peach and cherry,
a Concord grape vine. Strawberries.
A pussy willow stood in the corner,
behind which four friends and I
formed a club. Succulents grew
in the rock garden, tomatoes
and corn in the vegetable plot.

A silver lace vine created privacy
around the backyard's perimeter
as it knotted its way
through the wire fence.

To keep it all alive, my dad
constructed an extensive backyard
watering system. Well water
was the only game in town.

Within view of the kitchen window,
my dad built a drinking fountain.

A knob on the vertical pipe
turned the water on and off,
and from a small curved spout
water arced into a metal bowl.

My brother and I
discovered that the spout
was the perfect size and shape
for filling water balloons.

Over the Fence

Dad acquired our swingset
from someone who wanted to be rid
of it. That's how quite a few toys
came into our possession.

The swingset was a simple
but solid construction—a sun-faded
red steel pipe across the top and
a faded red A-frame support on each side,
each one with an aqua crossbar
over which a girl could fling her torso
and flip without her head hitting the earth.
The supports were buried into
the ground a ways, but not deeply
and not cemented in, so we couldn't
swing with wild abandon, couldn't swing
so hard that we would loop ourselves
around the top bar like cartoon characters.

Two wooden seats hung from chains.

My brother and I found that if one of us sat
on a swing facing the alley,
which was twenty feet away,
and the other rolled a ball toward the "batter,"
sometimes we could kick that ball over
the vine-covered fence.

A home run.

Shiny Crowns

At the Vickers gas station,
the pop machine sat outside
on the concrete stoop.
Ten cents for a bottle of pop.
The machine had a built-in opener
with a small container beneath it
to catch the bottle caps.

It didn't catch them all.

Scattered across the dirt and sand driveway
in front of the gas station was a galaxy
of shiny crowns: Pepsi, Dr Pepper, 7-Up,
Orange Crush, Coca-Cola.

Vickers was the jackpot for bottle caps,
but you could find them on any street
in town. Some whole, most flattened,
glints of red or blue or green
floating in a sea of sand.

Carris's Grocery

The grocery store was where I often spent
my nickel-per-week allowance. Eunice or one
of her teenage daughters listened
as my friends and I debated our candy choices
until finally we exchanged coins for cavities.

I'd often grab a Chick-O-Stick,
a box of Hot Tamales, or spend a penny
on a long lace of red licorice
that had been touched already
by who knows how many people.

The screen door
with its Rainbo Bread push bar,
and the wood-framed glass door
led to an old wooden floor
with narrow aisles of canned goods,
milk, bread, a few vegetables, limited choices—
your typical 1970s small-town grocery store.

The meat counter at the back
was Glen's purview, elevated a few feet
so the glassed-in case was eye level for a kid
inhaling the blood smell of freshly cut meat.
A small wooden ramp to the side
was the entry point on which to stand
to get Glen's attention for sliced bologna
or a pound of hamburger,
or for my friend Marilyn to ask if he'd make
a photocopy of sheet music for her.
Photocopies were an inky voodoo

we had not known before, and Glen
owned one of these machines.

Outside, the north wall had an unusual feature,
a built-in bench of sorts.
The building swooped out about a foot
off the ground, just for a little ways,
a long-enough bench for three or four kids
to sit on and chatter and laugh
while tying knots in our red licorice laces.

My Alaska Purchase

With a nickel
and three pennies
clenched inside my fist
I walked my 7-year-old self
down the sandy alley to the post office.
Reaching up and dropping my coins
on the counter, I told Roger
I wanted to purchase a stamp
for my collection.

He showed me several options,
and I walked away with
a rectangular Air Mail stamp
costing me the entire eight cents.
It was brown with a totem pole
on it along with the words
"Alaska Purchase."

My father had started me off with
a few colorful stamps
as well as a small stamp-collecting book
with a plastic spiral spine.

One Sunday afternoon each month, my dad,
brother, and I climbed the echo-y staircase
inside the Eagles building in Great Bend
to a room where we sat around tables

filled mostly with men and a few women.
Conversations about stamps were mostly over
my head, but there were always cookies.

None of the other stamp collectors
brought their kids to the meetings.
Leon and I were the lucky ones.

.

No Loitering

On the door of the
Pawnee Rock Post Office,
a sign: No Loitering.

Seriously?
Because that's all anyone ever did there.

Weekdays, one person after another
would lean against the counter,
telling Roger, the postmaster,
their views of the world
or bringing up their latest issue
with our city government.
Once talked out with Roger,
the person might move
to the freestanding table
and converse with others
stopping in to pick up their mail.

When the lobby's service window was closed
in the evenings and on weekends,
my friends and I found sanctuary there
on cold or rainy days.

Radiators under the east and south
plate-glass windows were topped
with upholstered cushions
made of aqua vinyl.
If the post office didn't want 8-year-olds
to idle there, then why provide seating,
we reasoned.

We familiarized ourselves
with the shadowy faces of the
FBI's Most Wanted, flyers
hanging on the post office wall.
A bank robber might just pass through
our town, you know, and we
eagle-eyed young citizens
would match face to flyer,
turn him in,
justify our loitering.

The Salt Plant Whistle

The Flintstones was one of the cartoons
       Major Astro aired on his TV show, which
beamed to our outside antenna
from a Wichita station. My brother and I
watched on the 13-inch black-and-white Zenith
in our basement after school.

When Fred Flintstone's workday was over
at Slate Rock and Gravel you knew it,
because a whistle blew—well, on the show
it was a bird that sounded.

Our town had a whistle,
a mechanical whistle, not a bird,
at the salt plant located just north of town,
next to the Pawnee Rock cemetery.

Depending on the direction of the wind,
we could usually hear
that whistle blow. Until it didn't.
Until Cargill, the company that pulled salt
out of the earth, closed the plant down
for good in the late '60s.

Adam, the father of my friend Amy,
worked nights at the salt plant,
but when they closed he had already
switched jobs, working now at Doerr's
in Larned, building stock tanks.
Adam carpooled to Larned,
and the man who rode with Adam

was a smoker. One day Amy and I,
probably 8 and 9, sneaked
into her dad's pickup, into his ashtray,
and found a butt with a bit of tobacco
left on it. Armed with kitchen matches,
we took the cigarette butt
behind her chicken house and lit it.

But we were not impressed,
and we did not pick up the habit. Not that
there was a chance in the world
our parents would have let us smoke.

Clutter Lindas Lumber Company—Since 1878

About the same time Amy and I
decided to become nonsmokers, we built
a pretend grocery store in her backyard.
We had acquired a cabinet—
two side-by-side wooden boxes
with hinged doors.
Amy and I decided we needed
a padlock to secure our
treasures within the cabinet.
We pooled our money
and walked to the lumberyard.

A small padlock with two keys cost
us a little more than a dollar—which
was big money, but we *needed* a lock.

That padlock may have been
my only purchase from Bill at the
Clutter Lindas Lumber Company—
a pretty minimal contribution
considering the countless hours my friends
and I perched rent-free on the bench in front
of his lumberyard.

Dirt Clod Physics

"Sit down.
    Don't get up.
Don't move around."
Those were the rules
for riding in the bed
of my dad's old Chevy pickup.

Dad sometimes let Leon and me
ride in the back on the way home
from the cemetery.

The bed was wooden
and often held a few clods,
a product of moving excess soil
from a fresh grave to the
cemetery's dirt pile.

Riding in the bed down the hill into town,
my brother and I liked
to toss these dirt clods
straight up in the air,
and we watched with amazement
as they fell behind
our moving truck
instead of landing in its bed.

Childhood is mostly
one lesson in physics
after another.

We learned how speed
and distance and time
made the dirt clod fall
on the pavement behind us.

Everything we did
came with those lessons
of trial and error:
how to pedal fast enough
to keep a bicycle upright,
how hard to toss a ball
to get it across home plate,
how quickly to let go
of firecracker
with a sizzling fuse.

Patches

She was the beloved dog
of our childhood—
a white rat terrier with brown ears.
She looked something like
the RCA dog, Nipper.

We got her from the Schraeders, who lived
down the street. Virgil helped
my dad dig graves, and his family had a litter
of puppies to give away.

The first night we had Patches,
she escaped from her pen and ran home
to the Schraeders. They called the next
morning while we were frantically
looking for her.

Patches was officially Leon's dog,
but she followed me anytime I left
the house.

The townspeople knew that
if Patches was sitting outside
of the grocery store or the post office
or the library, Cheryl was inside.

One day I went in the front door
of Marilyn's house; Patches bided
her time, sleeping on the porch.
I forgot about Patches and left
through Marilyn's back door.

When I got home, no Patches.
I had to go back and get her.
She was waiting for me
on Marilyn's front porch.

The Pawnee Rock Braves

I didn't go to watch the basketball game.
The game was the cause of the gathering;
I was after the effects—the social energy.

I was there to mingle with my friends
outside of class, to stare at Rodney,
maybe to joke around with him.

I was there to dream of being
like Jyl Behrens, a cheerleader.
I didn't necessarily want to lead cheers,
but I craved that uniform, the well-made royal blue
sweater with the gold letter "P" sewn on
its back, the heavy wool skirts,
royal blue with gold inserts.
White bobby socks and oxfords.
Long hair and a never-ending smile.

I was there for the show—for when the
cheerleaders took the court for their
long cheers with cartwheels and splits
at the quarter breaks,
to hear our band blast from the stands
across the court, to wheedle a dime
from my dad at halftime so I could
buy a bag of popcorn at the concession stand
in the school lunchroom.

After the game, I would find my dad.
My brother, who was actually watching the game,
would find Dad, too. And the three of us
walked the two and a half blocks
home together in the dark
on a cold January night.

Our Mid-Century Home

My dad loved old things.
History. Rusted iron. The old ways.

And yet, the house he built
in the early '60s
for his family to live in
had the features and stylings
of the modern world.

The interior offered long, sleek lines.
One wall of the living room
was covered with wood paneling—
a bright, reflective wood, seamless
(not the dreary dark paneling
of the '70s). Staggered shelves
covered most of this wall, a place
for books and objects,
with an angled display shelf
for magazines. Along the top
of the paneled wall, the length
of the room, was a wooden trough
for recessed lighting. Fluorescent
bulbs hidden inside flickered
and then came to life.

The focal point:
a brass-colored clock
built into the wall, as if it
had forced itself through
the paneling.

There were no numbers
on this clock to help a kid
learn how to tell time,
only rectangular metal pieces
in place of the 12, 3, 6, and 9,
circles for everything else.
Three hands swept across its face
measuring our lives
in this house by the hour,
the minute,
the second.

The Details

When you're a kid the things around you
become your normal, and you might take
them for granted.

But even as a youngster, I noticed the extra
touches that my dad put into our house
and the things he made.
He was an artist in disguise.

The Mennonite way of life,
at least through my eyes,
was simple, unadorned, and
leaned toward stark.
Anything done with a flair
or a lot of color seemed to be seen
as a waste of time, a misuse
of one's resources.

Our church had no ornamentation,
save a red neon light glowing beneath
a wooden cross hanging behind
the pulpit.

[The first time I stepped
into a Catholic Church at age 18,
I was in disbelief—a dozen statues,
paintings on the wall
(Stations of the Cross),
brilliantly colored

stained-glass windows with angels
and saints—and then layers of gold
and ornamentation on the altar.
I was a little freaked out, to tell you the truth.]

In my tiny hometown of blue-collar workers,
there was not much in the way of art
in homes. Many had pictures cut from calendars
framed and hung on a wall.

So until he hit his mid-40s, my dad's art
tended to show up in subtle ways, mostly in his
woodworking craftsmanship but also
in the details of our house.

Out the back door, Dad installed
wide wooden panels between
our yard and the neighbor's,
a bit of privacy for us.
These panels were each painted
a different color—pinks and greens,
yellows. With a redwood-stained
frame and a corrugated fiberglass roof
to keep our bikes and the doghouse dry.

The front porch was concrete, but it was tinted
red. Instead of a regular sidewalk, Dad
laid flat stones in a curved walk,
cementing the space between the stones
with the same red concrete.

After he retired, Dad would point out
found objects in his backyard,
and would tell me all the things
he wanted to make with them.
I knew he would run out of time
before he'd ever run out of ideas.

Fourth Grade

In fourth grade I began planning
my life. I would marry Rodney
and we would live in Pawnee Rock
forever.

Rodney had all the best qualities:
a fast runner, smart, funny.
During class he'd take a comb
from his pocket to pull his brown hair
straight down toward his face and then, holding
his hand over the bangs, use the
teeth-edge of the comb to swish the ends
to the right side. Dreamy.

I would become a novelist. And a scientist
of some kind, maybe a biologist
bent over a microscope. Or a meteorologist
studying icy clouds. And I'd be a detective,
unspooling the many mysteries of my neighbors.
I was curious about how all things worked.

In truth, I didn't get out much.
We went to Great Bend and Larned
for groceries and swimming.
My brother and cousins and I spent weeks
during the summer on my grandmother's farm.
We drove to Arkansas to visit my
maternal grandparents. But mostly,
I studied the movement of ants, searched

our clover for a stem with four leaves,
pedaled my bike endlessly around town.

I couldn't imagine
a greater place to live than where I was.
All of my friends were here.

The Red Miniskirt

On the day that my dad took
11-year-old me to the Emergency Room
in Larned to have a bite checked out,
I was wearing my favorite skirt, which
was as close to a miniskirt as the school
would allow.

I had awakened with a possible spider bite
and Dad's schedule was more flexible
than Mom's, so after Dad finished
the school bus route, he and I
made my first-ever visit
to the Emergency Room.

The doctor didn't seem too concerned.
"Keep an eye on it" was his advice.

The skirt was new, at least to me,
and I wasn't at all, normally, a
skirt-wearing girl, but miniskirts
were hippie fashion and I wanted to be in on that.
Plus, there was the benefit that short skirts
made the teachers nervous.
Our fourth-grade teacher made us girls kneel
on the floor while she used a ruler
to measure from the ground up.
The dress code stated that
dresses and skirts could be no higher
than 4 inches above the knee.
Finally, being short was to my benefit.

The skirt was pretty much
two pieces of cloth sewn together
with darts at the waist and a few belt loops,
a zipper in the back. It was
a deep red denim-like fabric
with very tiny white and yellow
flowers scattered about.

I didn't buy the skirt; it was a prize I
uncovered at the Larned City Dump,
back when the city dumps were filled
with usable but unwanted belongings,
before yard sales became a Saturday morning
tradition. I sometimes accompanied my dad
on his dump runs, and we'd dig through
cardboard boxes and find all kinds of treasures.
The red skirt was in a box. I held it up to my waist.
It looked like it would fit, so I took it home
and washed it.

And who knows, maybe a spider came home
with us, too.

Our Volunteer Fire Department

When the fire siren blared
we knew to stay out of the street.
The cavalry was coming.

Once the siren rang, it might be
30 seconds, maybe 60, before
cars and pickups would round
the corner, sliding to a stop
on the sandy street
in front of our house,
men bailing out of cars and pickups,
giving little attention to shutting
the doors behind them,
sprinting for the fire station
next door to our house.

The first guy in would
push up the garage door,
scribble the location and type of fire
on the chalkboard, and then—watch out
because that old fire truck was gonna
be blasting out of the building,
its wind-up siren screaming away,
red bubble light on its roof
spinning like a top.

The Ralph Wallace Cafe

It was like going to Sunday dinner
at Grandma's house, but without
all the pesky relatives.
A steaming buffet of fried chicken,
mashed potatoes and cream gravy,
green beans, Jell-O, dinner rolls,
pie, cake, pudding.

The Ralph Wallace Cafe
in downtown Great Bend
had at least three wood-paneled
dining rooms which were
always full and buzzing—
the jingle of silverware,
the waterfall of iced tea
being poured into a glass,
the clash of thick china
as tables were bused,
the hum of conversations,
a too-loud laugh.
On a wall of one room
hung banners of the Lions,
the Rotary, of all the groups
that met there.

This was the '60s and our family
didn't dine out often, maybe a couple
of times a year, and there was nothing
grander than standing in line,
inhaling those aromas,
then finally, finally, filling a plate.

Joe and Janet

Joe and Janet Bowman rode around Pawnee Rock every single night—at least during the warm months. They drove past our house in their white Buick or Oldsmobile or whatever it was, a family car, two kids bopping around in the backseat. Joe and Janet each had an elbow out the window, getting some air. Every single evening. Or afternoon if it was Sunday. You could count on it. Their car crept by, tires crunching on the sand. I suppose if you wanted to know what was going on in town, you could ask Joe and Janet.

⌒

My family took our first real vacation when I was 11. Colorado: Estes Park, Rocky Mountain National Park. As a flatlander kid, I was in complete awe. I had seen photographs of mountains, but my god, seeing them in person took my breath away. I was in love with the mountains.

Toward the end of the trip, we went up Pike's Peak and then visited the Air Force Academy outside of Colorado Springs. After touring the chapel, we drove on the exit road toward the highway.

While sitting at the stop sign behind other traffic, I watched cars turning into the Academy's campus.

One white car was familiar. I looked at the occupants. It was Joe and Janet Bowman. From Pawnee Rock.

We were 500 miles from home, on our first vacation ever, and we saw people from Pawnee Rock. Joe and Janet.

"Leon, look!" I said. "There's Joe and Janet. Here. Joe and Janet." Leon nodded.

"That was Joe and Janet Bowman," I told my parents in the front seat. They kind of shrugged, "Oh."

I don't think they believed me.

While no one else in our car recognized the marvelous juxtaposition of abnormal and normal of this Joe and Janet sighting in Colorado, I did. While seeing them in Colorado was totally unexpected, there they were: cruising slowly in their white car, windows down, two kids bopping around in the backseat.

A Picture Paints
a Thousand Words

The photograph,* likely taken
in the '70s, shows a brick building,
the word GARAGE embedded
in a concrete rectangle near the top.

The driveway that angles through
the north part of the building
provided a roof to gas pumps
that once stood there, servicing two lanes.
As a kid, I bicycled around and around
this now-empty concrete island,
pretending to stop to "fill 'er up."

The right side of the front of the building
was my dad's woodworking shop with three
plate-glass windows. After vandals broke
the windows a few times, he boarded
them up instead of replacing the glass.

As you stand in the street facing the shop,
in front of the far right window
you'll see a stump where a huge elm stood
during my childhood. The elm
offered afternoon shade to my dad's shop
and watched over a ditch (which was replaced
by curb and gutter in the '60s).

* See photograph on page 83.

Farther to the right, see that passageway
between buildings? One day
in my early teens,
while hanging out with friends
near the elevator, one of the boys
picked up a handful of wheat
from the ground and threw it
at a car passing by. The driver
slammed on his brakes to chase us down.
Adrenaline surged through my body.
"Shit!" We might die, I thought.
And we ran,
ducking between buildings.

The driver, alcohol on his breath,
grabbed Marilyn and yelled at her
until an older Pawnee Rock teen
driving by saw what was happening
and made the man release her.

And there, on the left side of the photo,
where you see an evergreen down the block—
that's where Marilyn and Sarah lived.

That tiny glimpse of a tree,
in the yard of a house that no long stands,
will write a hundred stories in my mind.

Population 1,200

When I was in junior high
my dad told me the population
of Pawnee Rock in the late 1800s
had been about 1,200 residents.

How could our town possibly
have had 800 additional people?

Dad showed me old photos of Centre Street
as proof—a row of buildings
filling up a block.

In contrast, our downtown around 1970
had more vacant lots than structures
and "thriving" was not how anyone
would describe it.

In the olden days, the town boasted
two general stores, an apothecary,
the *Pawnee Rock Herald,*
and numerous other businesses.

During my years in Pawnee Rock
I longed for activity, stores or cafes,
some sense of aliveness.
Other than high school
football and basketball games,
Pawnee Rock had no big gatherings
save one: on the second Saturday
of December, Santa Claus

came to town. A crowd showed up
and huddled together against the cold
while Santa handed out candy to the kids.

The best day of the year.

Up on the Rock

My friends and I often rode our bikes
to the Rock. We stood up
to pump the pedals
around the steep, circular drive.
Parking our bikes on the rocky ground
near the pavilion, we raced up the spiral
staircase to the top.

From there, we could see grain elevators
at Seward and Radium, the water tower at Larned,
and on a good day we could see Rozel
at 25 miles and the Burdett water tower
standing 32 hazy miles away.

Much of the Arkansas River Valley
was flat land. A line of trees, cottonwoods
mostly, outlined the river two miles south.

We climbed around this Dakota sandstone mound
for hours, reading the names and dates carved
in it by travelers passing through.

We were never alone. One car
after another pulled off US 56,
the Santa Fe Trail route, drove
through town, and stopped at the Rock
for the history and the view.

One summer morning before sunrise,
friends and I walked the quarter mile

to the Rock lugging food, matches,
and a cast iron skillet. A growling dog
lunged from a yard
but Debbie brandished the skillet
and the dog backed away.
On the hill we gathered twigs,
started a fire. The flames
weren't consistent
and our French toast was soggy,
but we tasted
adventure in every bite.

Popcorn

The TV set was kept in the basement—
on the countertop of the former kitchen,
next to the sink that my dad now
used for shaving.

Seating was a matter of hierarchy.
Leon, my elder, always had first choice
in everything—which end of the kitchen table
(next to the back door),
which side of the backseat
(behind the driver),
so Leon claimed the best chair in the basement—
the rocker. When Dad dragged home a beastly
green vinyl recliner, the rocker was demoted
and it became my chair.

So then, Leon took the recliner,
I now had the rocker
with its itchy straw padding,
and Dad sat on the piano bench
or sometimes on the folding chair
at the sewing machine
because that was a dad thing to do.
Comfort was not his style.

Dad watched whatever we kids watched
and we kids watched whatever Leon
wanted. Dad did like *Bonanza,* though,
and *The Red Skelton Hour.*

Some nights Dad made popcorn.
He'd pop a big batch on the stove,
pour it into a large paper grocery bag,
cut off the top half of the bag,
shake in a bunch of salt,
and bring it downstairs with some bowls.
Leon and I scooped
our bowls into the bag, filling them.
Whatever we didn't eat, Dad would.
No food went to waste
around my father.

Summer Evenings

Sitting on my front porch,
I yearned toward the tennis court
a half block away.
The big kids gathered there
on summer evenings,
"Crystal Blue Persuasion" blasting
from a car speaker,
the two doors of the Impala open
like wings.

Seven or eight cars nosed in,
facing the tennis court. But no one
swung a racket or hit a ball;
kids were standing, sitting on the benches,
perched on car hoods,
talking, shouting, laughing, smoking,
drinking, flirting.
Or whatever it was that teenagers did.
From my porch, I could only imagine.

Karma's Gonna Get You

I came home
from junior high one day
to discover a used
John Lennon record sitting
on top of my small stack
of 45s. The only one
who would've put it there
was my dad; he was a rummager,
always finding treasures,
and he probably thought:
"Hey, it's a record. My daughter
listens to a lot of music.
She'll like it."

"Did you put this record
in my room?" I asked.
"No, I didn't," he said.

Neither my brother
nor my mother put it there.

I was pretty sure that
my dad was fibbing,
and I couldn't figure out
why he'd lie
about something
as trivial as this.
In my 13-year-old mind,
his denial meant that someone
had broken into our house

and placed this particular record
in my room,
which spooked me,
left a creepy feeling in my gut,
kept me wide eyed, aware.

The song on the record
was "Instant Karma."

I had no idea what karma was.

But apparently it
(and maybe someone)
was out to get me,
and soon I could be dead.

Machete Work

During my teenage years, I took
jobs with local farmers each August.
I rogued milo, walking down the rows
of a field and cutting out the tall stalks
that would bind up a combine.

The summer before ninth grade,
I told Dad I had a job
in the milo fields and asked him if he
had a machete. He drove to Grandma's
barn, pulled one off her wall and
sharpened it for me. And gave me
all the dad-appropriate warnings
for machete handling. He insisted
I wear a long-sleeved shirt,
despite the heat, said that milo leaves
would slice open skin.

The long-sleeved shirt was hot,
but I was sure glad to have it.

1975

The mower shed,
small, white, and wooden,
sat tucked away among the cedars
in the northwest corner
of the cemetery.

Inside the shed
the riding mower rested
when it was off duty,
with its lingering odor
of gas and oil,
grass clippings scattered
on the wooden floor.
Shelves held an array of vases
which had been abandoned
on the cemetery grounds
weeks after the post–Memorial Day
cleanup. On the floor sat
a stack of temporary bronze markers
with names and dates
of the deceased—placeholders—
used until a headstone was installed.

I was 14 in 1973, and one spring day
I stepped into the opened shed—
Dad out on the mower—
and my eyes happened to fall
upon one of those markers.
He had removed
bronze letters and numbers

from other markers
and created one with his name.
He scheduled his year of death: 1975.

The bones in my legs dissolved.

Did my father plan to die
by his own hand in two years?
If so, would it be
before my brother graduated
from high school that year?
Or after?

Was my dad just playing around
with the marker,
his attempt at graveyard humor?

Decades later, I mentioned
that grave marker to my brother.
He had seen it, too.

On Ladders

I have a photo
of my father near the top,
on the 21st rung,
of a bowing-in-the-middle
wooden extension ladder.
He's reaching up and out,
painting the upper trim
of a two-story office building
in Larned.

A second ladder was laid
on its edge on the sidewalk,
one end braced against the wall,
the other end braced against
the ladder he was on.
A rope tied around the bottom
rung was secured somehow
on the building
to keep the ladder from slipping
out from under him.

Precarious at best.

Off Ladders

I walked into our house
in the middle of the day
and there my dad was,
sitting in his chair.

My dad was never at home
in the middle of the day,
and if he was he certainly
wasn't sitting in his chair—
he'd be out doing something.

"Your dad broke his heels, Cheryl,"
he said quietly.

At 16, it had never occurred to me
that breaking one's heels was even possible.

He had been working that day
at Mrs. Carpenter's house, on a ladder.
As the ladder began to fall, Dad leaped
for safety but landed on his feet
on the paved driveway.

Someone must have taken him
to the hospital or to the doctor
and brought him home.

Dad refused the wheelchair that Mom
borrowed. Instead, he crawled on hands
and knees around the house,
up and down the stairs.

With Mom at work during the day,
it was up to me to drive Dad to Larned
for a follow-up doctor's visit.

When you're a teen, pretty much
everything about your parents
embarrasses you, but getting out
of Dad's truck that day,
my dad on his hands and knees,
crawling into the doctor's office,
I was embarrassed for myself,
but I felt even worse for him.

A Fine Dog

The summer before my senior year
of college, my mom called to say
that our dog, Patches, was in her last days.

I went home that July afternoon
and stayed awake all night,
sitting on the living room floor,
petting Patches and telling her
what she had meant to me,
to all of us.

I needed something tangible,
so I plucked some of her
white hair and put it in an envelope.
Because what else can you save of a dog,
besides memories?

She didn't make it through the night.

When my parents got up at dawn,
I asked Dad, "Can you help me
carry Patchie outside?"
Dad dug a grave in the backyard
near the bamboo, and I laid her body
in the ground. Dad and Mom and I
stood there, looking at the mound of dirt,
a world of grief stuck in our throats.

Education
by Happenstance

Other than it was scaly,
that it flaked off occasionally,
and brought shame,
I didn't know a thing
about my dad's skin
and his sister's skin.

My dad didn't have a treatment plan,
so maybe he never had a diagnosis.
Or maybe his doctor told him
it was just one of those
"you have to live with it" ailments.

My dad had a form of ichthyosis,
but I didn't know that at the time.
I didn't have a name for it until
my senior year in college when I
attended an end-of-semester
gathering at a professor's home.
On the way to the restroom,
I passed through her dining room
where a clipped, lone newspaper article
on the table caught my eye.

The article, with its overview
of the malady, provided information
I'd wondered about my entire life.

Answers sometimes come
from the most unexpected places.

A GUST OF WIND

My dad's woodworking shop.

Revival

Following my parents' divorce,
my dad, then in his mid-50s,
went on a spiritual quest of sorts.
Having grown up in the Mennonite faith,
he was looking to see
if he fit in anywhere else.

We were taking a drive when he told me,
"I went to a Black revival last week."

He stopped for an intersection,
then proceeded with his story.

"A Black woman invited me.
She insisted I give her a ride.
When I went to pick her up,
I was surprised to meet her husband.
He was an atheist, she told me.
I didn't know she was married,
and I didn't like the idea
of taking another man's wife somewhere.
But we went."

On the third night of the revival,
the minister asked him
to come up front and read scripture.
"I was nervous about reading in public,"
Dad told me. "I used to read to you kids
all the time. You were always

on our laps and we read to you,
but I was afraid to read out loud in public.

"Then the minister told us we had to hug
three people before we left."

Dad, driving, looked over at me,
caught my eyes and said,
"I had never hugged
a Black person before."

Dad Remarries

In the mid-'80s, several years
after my parents divorced,
my Dad began dating.

One woman, let's call her Sally,
was smart, open-hearted, friendly.
I was impressed.
Dad enjoyed her company
and she his. Dad brought her
to my house, and she invited me
to dinner at hers.

Then one evening, Dad, at 61,
called to tell me he was getting married—
in two weeks—to someone named Betty,
(not the same Betty who owned the tavern
in Pawnee Rock).

"Wait," I said. "What happened to Sally?"
He replied, "We weren't yoked right."

Red flags were going up all over my map.

I met Betty at their wedding.
She stood beside my dad at the altar,
her short hair a champagne-colored perm.
She wore an autumn-toned shirtwaist dress.
Betty seemed prim but was pleasant enough.

Still, I had reservations.

I thought no one would ever truly
"get" my dad, understand his oddities,
much less appreciate them.

You're Welcome Here Anytime

A month or so after Dad married Betty,
I drove to Pawnee Rock for a visit.
This was my childhood home,
the house my dad built around me,
the place I learned how to read
Go, Dog! Go, the home where I
spent the first 18 years of my life.
I could point out the loose strip of
Formica on the living room countertop,
knew how loud the click
of the hallway light switch was,
and I still had a few belongings
in the drawer under the table top
at "my place" at the kitchen table.

I had only met Betty once,
in the church on the day
she married my dad,
so I didn't have a good read on her yet.

During the visit when Betty said,
innocently enough,
kindly enough,
"You're welcome here anytime,"
my silent reaction was,
"This is my house. Of *course*
I'm welcome here anytime."

Yet in that moment,
a higher power must have
pulled rank; I held my emotions,
held my tongue.
I was touched by
some sort of non-Cheryl grace,
because I paused and
accepted her welcome,
gave her a chance.

Betty's Somersault

After a few years
of living with my dad,
Betty told me this story:
"Last week your dad
was in our bedroom
at his desk, looking over papers.
I wanted to see
if I could get a rise out of him
so I ran into the room
and did a somersault
onto the bed—and Elgie,
well, he just turned his head
reeeeal slowly and looked over at me,
his eyebrows up.
And he then turned back
to his papers
without saying a word."

She laughed. "That's your dad."

Everybody
Has a Backstory

When my dad remarried,
Betty jumped right in to help
with the yardwork.
She painted the white picket fence
that separated the front yard from the back;
Betty was a worker. In her 60s and 70s,
she'd be at the top of a ladder,
helping Dad paint the house.

Cutesy ceramic animals
also started showing up in the yard:
a turtle tucked among the day lilies,
a frog beneath the lilacs.
Betty was childlike
with her anthropomorphisms.
"See the turtle's big grin?
It's like he's bursting with good news."

Betty's stories
of childhood often looped back
to her family's home,
a one-room schoolhouse.
The interior was a wide-open room
with a chalkboard, and she'd tell how
she and her sisters roller skated
in an oval inside the house.
Her mother let them do things like that,
but when Betty mentioned her father,
her voice went low.

"He was a drunkard,"
was all she'd say about him.

Betty made a point to look
for the cheerful aspect in things
and on each visit I made,
she and Dad showed me what
they'd done in the yard.

Betty, her eyes twinkling,
pointed at a ceramic face and said,
"Look at that frog winking. See that?
He's got a story to tell."

Better Than Drano

It wasn't until Dad was in his 60s
that he found something of a fix
for his skin.

"I was unclogging
Doris Spreier's bathroom sink
and the Drano she had put in the pipes
splashed onto my arms
and it cleared my skin.
That gave me an idea. I wanted to
make a paste of Drano
and rub that on."

My entire body cringed.
"What? No. No. No. No.
You don't use Drano."

But then Betty jumped in to say,
"God led us to a skin doctor in Wichita
and he gave Elgie some Retin-A
and it's clearing up his condition.

"Well, you know that his mother
tried so hard to find something
to help him and his sister
and never could," Betty said.

(No, I didn't know how hard
Grandma had tried. We didn't
talk about Dad's skin
when I was a kid.)

"So we went to the nursing home
and Elgie rolled up his sleeves
and showed his mother his arms,"
Betty said, "but we don't know
if she understood."

A Dad Joke

D*ad:* That's where Moses was
when the lights went out.
Me: Where?
Dad: In the dark.

A Gust of Wind

A big gust of Kansas wind
at 3 o'clock on a Wednesday afternoon,
and the building, a seemingly permanent
fixture on Main Street, collapsed
into a pile of dust and bricks.

My dad started
his woodworking shop
in that building in 1948.
He worked there for 46 years.

He was in the process of retiring
and had already moved most
of his belongings out.

The timing was lucky.
He wasn't in his shop when it fell,
and no one from the adjacent business
was in the storage area of the building.

A gust of wind.

Blame It on the Sun

In early October, the Kansas sun
slices through the atmosphere
at an uncomfortable angle.
The slant at any time of day
in October is unsettling.
In the early morning,
it can blind an eastbound driver.

The driver is a friend of Dad and Betty's
and in all fairness, my dad probably crosses
the street in front of his house without looking
both ways as he heads off toward the alley on
his morning walk to the post office
to collect the mail.

On this morning in 1996, I am working as
a receptionist for an insurance agent in Emporia,
and am looking out the window
when my husband drives up.
The solemn expression on Dave's face
tells me that something is very wrong.

Dave just happened to be home
that morning and answered the phone
when Betty called
from the Great Bend hospital.

I close the office, pack an overnight bag,
and Dave and I race to Wichita.
We arrive at Wesley Medical Center
before the helicopter does.

The doctors let me have five seconds.
I touch my dad's arm as they roll him
toward emergency surgery.
He isn't conscious,
an ear chewed up.
He does not look good.
I wonder if he recognizes
my voice in the blur of nurses,
fluorescent lights, vanilla hallways.

The Unmet

After learning of my dad's accident,
before I head to Wichita,
I call my brother in Anchorage,
wake him up, tell him Dad is being flown
to Wichita, that he might not survive.

Leon, his wife,
and 5-month-old son fly in,
arrive at midnight,
prepared to say goodbye to our father,
if necessary, but if things work out,
Leon wants Dad to see his first grandchild,
wants Sam to meet his grandfather.

Faith

A hospital waiting room
ages you overnight.

It wisens you
as quickly as anything
to the fragility of life.

The hospital chaplain meets with us,
but there's no way his prayers
can measure up to the determined
prayers of my stepmother.

From the very first moment,
Betty lays out her will
to God and to us:
Elgie would receive
a full recovery.
Nothing less.

"When you've built and stored
your faith over the years,"
Betty tells me, "you have
a solid foundation to lean on
in times like this."

Waiting
Is the Hardest Part

In 1996, before Google,
before the Internet overflowed
with information,
I wanted better answers than
the vague ones the nurses provided
about comas, about the survival chances
of a 70-year-old with a closed-brain injury.

How long does a coma usually last?
Can my dad hear us?
Do our words register?
What makes a person awaken?
What if he never wakes up?
If he does wake up,
what will be his quality of life?

The first 24 to 48 hours are vital,
they say. During surgery a shunt
is inserted in his skull
to relieve pressure on the brain
but pressure is still a constant worry,
pneumonia a looming threat.

In the Surgical Intensive Care Unit,
we get to see my dad
for five minutes five times a day,
two family members at a time.
Each visit could easily be our last
chance to see him alive.

Time stands still.
My dad lies still.
There is not a fluttered eyelid,
no hands shifting,
no feet rearranging
the sheets.

In the Next Bed

After the first 85-hour day
of hanging out
in the Surgical Intensive Care Unit
and its waiting room,
you begin to feel seasoned,
you've become an old pro
at the schedule of visitations,
you've gained an understanding
of the soberness of the SICU.

Twelve beds in the long room,
six on each side,
each bed occupied by someone
walking that thin line
between life and death.

On the second morning,
at the 6 AM visitation,
the electronic doors open
and Betty and I enter with high hopes,
but Dad has not awakened.
Nothing has changed. Hope diminishes
quickly, shifts back to uncertainty.

On Day 5, while I'm at my dad's bedside,
a nurse comes to talk to a new patient,
a teenage boy in the next bed.
He's fresh out of surgery.

"You were in an accident," she tells the boy,
but he seems unconscious, unable to take

in any information. "You've had
a spinal injury. You're paralyzed."

During our next five-minute visit,
I see a man standing a ways back
from the bed where the teenager sleeps.

The man looks at me,
his eyes pleading. I recognize the feeling
of having gut-kicking emotions
and not knowing what to do with them.
I leave my dad's side and go to his.

"My son was in a car wreck last night,"
the man tells me. "He was driving.
His best friend was killed."
I lay my hand lightly on the man's shoulder
to ground him.

He tells me about receiving
the life-shattering news,
tells about his son being life-flighted,
tells about driving the dark highways
to Wichita.

I, myself, have just learned the iffiness
of recovery. I have no words
of comfort to offer.
All I can give him is my time,
my presence, my heart.

My Father's Arms

All things considered, my dad
looks pretty good for bouncing
off the grill of a moving pickup and landing
on one of the few paved streets in town.

One ear has been sewn back together,
and he has about twenty little knots
of black stitches sticking up out of his head,
where rocks or sand
had forced their way into skin.
His scalp has yellow splotches
from the Betadine.

Dad, whose mind is out cruising
in another dimension,
is wearing a hospital gown.

Because of his skin condition,
Dad had always kept his skin hidden.
He never wore short sleeves.
No sandals and no T-shirts.
And for heaven's sake,
shorts were unthinkable.

Other than when he rolled up his long sleeves
a few turns, I had never seen his arms
much above his wrists.

But now, I see his collarbone.
His upper chest. His uncovered arms.
For the first time in my
37 years on the planet,
I see my father's bare arms.

Coma, Day Twelve

The days are the same
but with increasing anxiety.

I begin to ask how many years
can a human linger in the void
between worlds?

Pneumonia catches up with my dad
and new meds are given.
He doesn't move a muscle.

Betty stays fiercely hopeful
but my hopefulness has begun to lag.
My brother is still here from Alaska;
he's keeping me afloat.

The nurses tell us that next week
they will prepare him
for long-term care.

With each visit, I watch for any flicker
of movement. Nothing, nothing, nothing.

On Day 12, at the 5 PM visit,
the nurse tells us when she suctioned
Dad's mouth this afternoon,
he opened his eyes wide.

Leon, Betty, and I temper
our excitement; many are
suffering around us,
but our smiles are huge,
our hugs are happy ones.
Dad is finally headed
in the right direction.

Waking Slowly

The next day my dad's blue eyes
are open a tiny bit. A blank stare.
He is not taking anything in.

He does not meet my
waking-from-coma expectations,
drawn from watching actors on TV shows
awaken and immediately start conversing.

He is transferred
to the Medical Intensive Care Unit
in Wesley and recovers
a tiny bit each day.

His eyes begin to follow movement;
he begins to respond to voices.

I stand beside his bed. He is looking
right at me. "Hi, Dad. It's Cheryl."
As soon as I say those words,
he deliberately turns his head away,
looks the other direction.

I know he's not in his right mind.
But still, it stings.

That'll Be a No on the Juice

After five weeks at Wesley Hospital,
Dad is transferred by ambulance
to Central Kansas Medical Center
in Great Bend.

With Dad twenty minutes away,
Betty can sleep in her own bed again.

Dad is awake, but he is not
back to being himself.
Or, maybe he *is* back to himself—uncontainable.

He is a fall risk. He isn't clear-headed
enough to get out of bed on his own,
and yet he tries. The staff has to restrain him,
strap him to the bed.

"Am I in the penitentiary?" he asks me
with total sincerity.

He was kind of on point.

A nurse inquires his preferences
for an afternoon snack.
"Would you like juice?" she asks.

"Juice is for city girls," he says.

67 Days

On December 14,
after 67 days in the hospital,
after hours of rehab, recovery,
learning to walk again,
Dad makes it home.

Each day he is
a little brighter,
a little more with it.

His memory returns.

However, the traumatic brain injury
has crimped something in his head
making him more emotional.
His torso shakes as he tries
to contain tears when something
touches his heart.

Dad has made stellar progress
so after he gets home, I send
a thank-you letter with photos
to the SICU at Wesley Hospital.
I want the nurses and doctors
to see their work
made visible.

Dad eventually tosses aside
his walker. And before long,
Betty has him up
in front of the congregation
to offer their testimonials.

Betty had made it clear at the outset,
to God and everyone,
that she expected a full recovery.

She got one.

At the Edge

After Dad's traumatic brain injury,
he changed a bit. When your brain
bounces around inside your skull,
it shakes things up, and your mind
may begin to operate differently.

In some ways, my dad became
more accessible, more open,
a bit more emotional.

After that injury, he
began to share personal feelings—
which was something new—
and one day he mentioned
a memory that was obviously
from a period of depression.

When I was very young
there were a few weeks
that night after night, Dad
failed to come home at suppertime
and Mom would put Leon and me
in the car and we'd go "looking for Dad."

And we'd find him sitting in the dark
in his pickup, either at the cemetery
or at the Rock, where he took down
the flags each evening.

"I'd sit in my pickup at the edge
of the Rock," he tells me, talking about
those days forty years earlier.
"And I'd think about driving
my pickup over that edge."

It was a steep drop of about 20 feet,
which would've brought
a crash landing on rocks.

"I didn't do it though," he said.
"I was afraid I might live, but be injured.
And I didn't want someone
to have to take care of me."

It meant a lot to me that my father
trusted me enough to share
one of his darkest moments.

And his words confirmed that
some of my childhood fears were real,
not imagined.

By his being vulnerable,
what my dad handed me
was nothing less than a tender gift,
a moment of true connection.

A Well-Dressed Man

In one of the earliest photos
I have of my dad,
he's about 6 years old,
wearing overalls like all the other boys
in the picture. The back of the photo
says "Bible School."

(There was such a thing as Bible School
in the early 1930s?)

(Apparently. I guess I had assumed that
Bible School was a 1960s invention.)

During my childhood,
my dad was a carpenter,
a school bus driver,
a cemetery caretaker,
a substitute rural mail carrier,
and for all of those jobs,
the overalls worked just fine.

On Lions Club meeting nights, however,
Dad put on slacks, a nice shirt, nice shoes
to wear to meetings
held in the school lunchroom.

In his later years, Dad nurtured
his eccentricities, became more comfortable
talking to strangers. He'd encounter a man
wearing overalls, nod and say,
"Now there's a well-dressed man."

At War with the Crows

In a movie Dave and I
watched recently, the film opened
to a leafless tree on a hill,
a man and a shotgun.

The narrator said, "My father
was at war with the crows."

I smiled, remembering the time
I noticed the two red plastic jugs
my father kept near his back porch.
Laundry detergent bottles. Era brand.

Betty explained, "The bottles
have small rocks inside
and your dad tosses
them in the air
to scare crows away
from the birdfeeders."

She grinned, "I know the neighbors
must think he's nuts."

(See also: At War with the Squirrels)

At War with the Squirrels

My father had no love
for squirrels. They tested him,
outsmarted him at his bird feeders.

But whenever some sort
of homeowner's challenge
presented itself, Dad
figured out a way to fix it.

On one visit, I learned that Dad
had been capturing squirrels
(humanely) in a cage,
then marking their backs
with a dot of yellow paint
to later determine
if they were repeat offenders.
He and Betty drove each squirrel
two miles to the other side
of the Arkansas River
where he set them free.

"Squirrels can't swim,"
Betty said, explaining why
they released them across the river.

I don't know
if squirrels can swim or not,
but I'll bet they sure could run
across the bridge.

(See also: At War with the Crows)

Crossing the Street

L eon brought his sons,
  Sam and Nik, from Alaska
to visit Dad, now fully recuperated
from his near-death accident.
I joined them in Pawnee Rock
and we all went for a walk.

The Unruh herd left the safety
of the yard and stepped
into the street to cross it
at an angle, the way we always had,
headed for the alley.

Four years earlier, this had been
the spot where Dad got hit
by a pickup. But did our father
look both ways when he stepped out
into the street this time?

No, he did not.

LETTING TIME BE

Elgie Unruh in his Pawnee Rock home, 2005.

Life in a Small Town

"Howard has your turkey
in his freezer at the gas station,"
my dad said.

I processed that sentence
the best I could, but looked at Dad
for more information.

"I entered your name
in the Lions Club
raffle for a Christmas turkey
and you won."

One Saturday morning
each December,
Santa Claus rode down
from the Rock (North Pole)
on the fire truck.
After he handed out
sacks of candy to the kids,
Santa pulled names
from a chicken-wire hopper.

There was no room in
Dad's freezer for my turkey,
and Howard, faithful Lion,
offered to keep the turkey
for me in his freezer,
quietly nestled among the
Bomb Pops and Drumsticks.

When you move away from
a tiny town, you forget how relaxed
things are, how informal.

And you realize that Howard
and the other good
and decent adults looked out
for you when you were a kid
—and still do
when given the chance.

The Olden Days

"I'm part of the olden days,"
my father once told me.

Dad cherished the hundreds
of household and farm items he
accumulated over the years: things he
had saved from his parents' farm
and items he had gathered elsewhere.

This was the life he loved, the keeping
of the old things. He would sometimes offer
an object to me, but I could hear
the reluctance to let go in his voice
and I'd politely decline.

On visits to Pawnee Rock to see Dad,
we'd be in the backyard or his basement,
and Dad would pick up something,
maybe a four-foot piece of twirled copper
and ask Dave and me,
"Do you know what this is?"
When we shook our heads no, he'd say,
"That's a lightning rod
from your grandfather's barn."
Dad loved stumping us.
Another item would catch his eye
And he'd pick it up
and hold it for the pop quiz:
"Do you know what this is?"

This became something of a running joke,
so now when Dave and I wander
through an antique store,
I wait for Dave to raise
some peculiar object and ask,
"Do you know what this is?"

Letting Time Be

I doubt that my dad ever drove
a vehicle over 55 miles per hour.
He was never in a hurry.
And yet he arrived on time.

In his carpentry shop,
he varnished wood
and he waited
until it was completely dry
before sanding it,
before adding another coat.
He knew not to push things.

On summer evenings, he stood
in the yard with a hose,
watering the grass, the shrubs,
his flowers. He had sprinklers
to do the work for him, but he had
all the time in the world
to water the lawn.

A One-Man Promoter
of Pawnee Rock

My father made a replica of the Rock
and it sat high on a shelf in his shop
well out of reach of
grubby little paws like mine.

The pavilion Dad made
with the spiral staircase
looked pretty much like the one
at the state historic site just north of town.

Surrounding the pavilion
were red-colored rocks—
Dakota sandstone, like the ones on the hill.
Nearby was a replica of the monument
and a tiny flagpole flying the American flag.

After Dad retired from his job
as rural mail carrier,
he went on the parade circuit,
loading his mini version
of the Rock onto the back of his pickup.
His hand-painted sideboards announced:

> *Visit and See the Historic Rock*
> *at Pawnee Rock*
> *Famous Look Out Point*
> *Along the Santa Fe Trail*

I helped him set up at a few area parades.
During Ellinwood's After Harvest Festival,
the announcer introduced parade entries:
"Next up is Elgie Unruh. He's a one-man
promoter of Pawnee Rock."

The Santa Fe Trail

When the Model T car owners
organized a regional caravan
and planned a stop atop
Pawnee Rock State Historic Site
in 1991, my dad went into action.

He cut postcard-sized pieces
of thin wood, stamped them
with a line drawing of the Rock
and the name of the event.
He glued on a tiny piece of rock,
added a Lions Club sticker,
and handed them out
to the Model T drivers
and to other groups
passing through town,
a souvenir of the Rock's
place in Santa Fe Trail history.

My dad,
the One-Man Promoter
of Pawnee Rock.

Their Own Language

After a Saturday lunch buffet
at the Great Wall of China,
we left Great Bend, headed west
on Tenth Street Road
with Betty behind the wheel
of their Taurus.

From the passenger seat
Dad pointed casually to the right
then said to Betty,
"I think they built a pond out there."

Betty glanced back over the seat at me
and said, "And that's to tell me
I'm driving too fast."

She laughed.

"He doesn't
just come out and tell me
I'm driving too fast."

Always on the Road

My dad drove the school bus route
for 18 years, starting the year
my brother was born, ending
the year Leon left high school.

During those same years,
Dad had been the
substitute rural mail carrier,
filling in when Virgil Smith
was sick or on vacation.
When Virgil retired, my dad
took over the rural route.

The seasons came and went.
My parents divorced several years
after I left home and Dad
began using his weekends
to travel Kansas.
He set out to photograph
every county courthouse
as well as every post office
in the state.

When he married Betty,
she was more than happy
to go along on these weekend trips.

"When we're traveling, we stop
at convenience stores," she told me,
then leaning in with a grin,
as if sharing a secret,
"On these trips, we stop and I buy a bag
of crunchy Cheetos. It feels
like I'm getting away with something."

The Last Place
He'd Ever Want to Be

"Ella has lost some
of her knowledge,"
my dad told me once.
"Every time I go see her,
she's asleep. I don't wake
anybody up when I go to
the nursing home."

Ella was his mother's younger sister
and she lived to be 102.

After he retired, Dad visited
a nursing home in Larned each Tuesday.
On Wednesday mornings,
after drinking coffee with the old Mennonites
at Burger King, he visited friends
in the Great Bend nursing homes.

I can't know for sure my father's motives,
and maybe my own are sneaking in here,
but I think he was hedging his bets,
putting time in now in nursing homes,
so maybe he wouldn't have to later.

Apology

I suppose my dad apologized
to me more than once, but
I clearly remember the time
when, referring to his skin condition,
he said, "I'm sorry I couldn't do
all the things with you kids that
other dads did like go swimming
with you, take you to the pool."

"But you did so many other things
with us," I jumped in, mentioning
that he taught Leon and me how to fish
on the banks of Pawnee Creek,
how to hunt for fossils
at Kanopolis Lake,
how to skip stones
across the Arkansas River
when the river still had water in it.

I reminded him that
he lifted my brother and me onto his lap
when we were toddlers to read to us,
that he let us ride with him
on the school bus route,
that he took us to every home
high school football and basketball game.

My dad helped Leon and me
each build a bookshelf
at his woodworking shop,

taught us how to hammer a nail
without hitting our fingers,
how to pull a saw
straight back behind us.

I told him that he let us
watch him dig graves,
and that we even got
to help him when we got older.
Did any of my friends
get to dig graves with their dads?
No. Not a single one.
(Not legally anyway.)

I was probably 50 when my dad
made this apology—and even though
I protested his apology at the time,
I wish I had said more, convinced him
that he had not let me down.

And Now This Moment of Synchronicity

On one visit to see my dad and stepmother, Dad and I rummaged through boxes in his basement. I came across an old book, *Favorite Poems,* with a brown cloth cover. It was frayed on the corners and had my mom's name written in her hand on the inside cover. "Give that to your mother," Dad said.

Dad and I went upstairs to get ready for lunch. I laid the book on the living room counter and helped Betty set the table. She used paper towels for napkins and I folded each one in half. The paper towels had unattributed phrases printed on them.

A line printed on every other piece of towel was "And the song, from beginning to end, I found again in the heart of a friend." That sounds familiar, I thought, but couldn't place it. I read aloud the words on the paper towels to Dad and Dave as I set the table.

That chore complete, I picked up the book of poetry that I had, minutes before, discovered in Dad's basement. With Dad and Dave sitting on the living room couch, I opened the book with a dramatic flair to a random page and read aloud a poem.

The poem I opened to was "The Arrow and the Song" by Henry Wadsworth Longfellow. It ended with the very line appropriated by the paper towel company: "And the song, from beginning to end, I found again in the heart of a friend."

Walking Sticks

After his retirement from the post office,
Dad installed a small metal shed
in his backyard. He had some tools inside
and he stored wood,
mostly small tree branches.

So as not to create a mess
in the house, Dad sat on the stoop of the shed
and with his pocket knife chipped bark
off of branches. He'd clean away the bark
and sand the wood, then use
his "typewriter" (a punch kit),
hammering individual letters into the wood.
With ink pens, he colored the indentations.

He wrote Bible verses, jokes,
weird sayings that he found who knows where.
He signed his sticks "Elgie,"
which he occasionally shortened to "LG."
Near the bottom of the stick near his name
he stamped the name of the tree:
cherry, elm, cedar.

On one he punched in "Tree of Knowledge."
When I read that aloud, Betty said,
"In other words, he don't know what kind of tree."

The Move to Great Bend

I thought my dad would be
carried out of the house he built,
but he went willingly.

In the autumn of 2005,
without any warning,
Betty wrote to tell me they
had moved to an apartment
in Great Bend and in two weeks
they'd be auctioning
my childhood home
and the belongings inside
that they didn't take with them.

She said I could go to the house
and salvage things that meant
something to me.
I would've liked more notice,
but you get what you get.
I was in panic mode trying
to save family treasures.

I made two trips to Pawnee Rock,
rummaged through the house,
filled my car twice,
searched everywhere,
looked in all the secret nooks,
but I couldn't find the train set.

I scrambled to gather
the family and personal things,
historical Pawnee Rock documents
and photographs.

Although my father had made
a 96 percent recovery after his
near-fatal accident in 1996,
Betty had seen Dad's diminished ability
to do the mowing and the house painting
and I'm sure she didn't want to be caught
with a house full of stuff if he died.
Dad's basement space was orderly,
but full.

However, she waited until Dad,
then 79 years old,
was onboard with leaving the house,
and she quickly made her move.

She made the right call for them.
I just wish I'd had more notice.

The Auction

Psychological torture
and deep emotional scarring
were a featured personal event
at the auction of my childhood home.

I'd had only a few hours in the house
the week before the auction
to pick out things I wanted.
I didn't have the chance
to sort through much.
And there was so much.

But there we were. Auction day.

Larry Carr, a second cousin,
was the auctioneer, and he was
very kind to me that day,
checking in to make sure
I was OK, even though I wasn't.

When I had arrived that morning,
Larry approached me and said,
"When my staff was cleaning
out the house, we found six
coffee cans full of coins under
the bed in the basement.
They're in the cab of my truck.
Let me get them for you."

On the auction tables, I couldn't find
the heavy, metal train set
that I intended to grab for my brother.
Later, I saw it being auctioned off
at a price higher than I had money for.

My Girl Scout knife went for $15.
I'd have kept it had I seen it
before the auction.

In the yard, I found the dresser
that had been in my bedroom.
Still taped to the frame of the mirror
were things I had posted there
during my teenage years,
one of which was a tiny
black-and-white photo
of Alan Alda, from *M*A*S*H,*
a favorite TV show.

I ripped the photo from the dresser
as the crowd built around me.
"They may get everything else,"
I said to myself,
"but they're not getting Alan Alda."

Farmers Caps

After they moved to Great Bend,
my dad still made
his walking sticks.
With his pickup door open,
he'd sit in the passenger side
of his truck in the apartment building
parking lot and chip away at the bark.

When he quit driving
and they sold the pickup,
Dad still created.
He used what he had.
And what he had, apparently,
was an abundance
of seed caps that farmers wear,
and caps from the local co-op.

So Dad bought a hot-glue gun
and small plastic figures
from the hobby store
and glued things onto
the bills of a dozen caps,
creating dioramas
of cowboys and horses,
of cattle and corrals,
of ham bones and nickels.
He was nothing
if not resourceful.

He'd wear one of these caps
when we'd eat Saturday lunch
at the Great Wall of China.

Flight Risk

My dad was not one to be contained,
but he was falling down a lot
and was no longer able to get up.
Betty would have to call for assistance.
Sometimes the manager
of the apartment building
was the one who lifted him
off the floor.

Dad's lack of balance
and increasing Alzheimer's symptoms
were becoming more than Betty
could handle.

He was in the hospital after his last fall
and Betty said the doctor would
recommend he be moved
to a nursing home.

I didn't want to be around
when Dad got that news.

When I visited him in the hospital,
I don't think he'd been told yet,
but somehow he knew; he was ready to bolt.
His hospital room was on the ground floor.
The outside door was in sight.

He looked at me and asked,
"Where's your car?"

Fading Out

One of my dad's favorite things
to do on my visits to their apartment
was to bring out his albums
of old Pawnee Rock photos,
point out the people and identify them.

Then, the last year or so,
with an album on my lap, I'd ask,
"Who's that?" and more and more
he'd say, "I don't know."

Then he started not fully tracking
with the conversation in the room.

And then they put my dad
in a locked Alzheimer's wing
of a nursing home.

Knowing how much my dad
hated the thought of ending his days
in a nursing home, my drive
from Emporia to Great Bend
that day in July of 2011
was agonizing.

In the red-brick nursing home
with its long hallways of gloom,
I found my dad in a living room–like
area with a dozen other people.

I got permission from the nurse
to bring in food, so
I made a run to KFC. He's always
loved fried chicken. He ate it up.

A nurse told me that when
Dad had been transferred
from the hospital the day before,
they put him
in general population.
He tried to make a run for it,
exit the building.
That's when
they locked him in.

On my drive home
that first day,
I imagined my dad
breaking out,
finding a wooded area,
sitting on the grass,
leaning against a tree,
taking his last breath there.

And if it happened that way,
I would be OK with that.

Nursing Home, Day 10

Betty called. Dad had been
transported from the nursing home
to the hospital. He was having
trouble breathing.

I drove to Great Bend and when I
walked into his hospital room,
his skin was gray.
He was asleep. His spirit
seemed like it had withdrawn.

My initial thought was
"This is a person who will not
make it through the day."

Thinking it was his last day,
I said all the words I needed to say,
standing there by his side
while he was sleeping
or out taking a tour of the next world.

But my dad, always the comeback kid,
gradually perked up.
He looked at me, and for the first
time in weeks seemed to really
know who I was. He smiled. His
eyes recognized me. He called me
by name.

He made a comment about the
"Kansas" T-shirt I was wearing.

Betty showed up for a while;
she had been home resting
and then she left early. So Dad
and I had the afternoon together.

When the nurse brought in his supper
at 5, he chowed down his sandwich
and applesauce. Cleaned his
plate. He looked alive!

He'd be all right for now.
I felt strong enough in my belief
that I said my goodbyes
and drove home to Emporia.

Five minutes after I walked
in the door, the phone rang.
The nurse told me
my dad was gone.
His spirit had left this world.

The Shovel

In the corner of my bedroom closet
is my father's shovel, the blade
rectangular and flat
with a square-bottomed edge.

When he was in his 30s and 40s,
my father hand-dug dozens,
perhaps hundreds, of graves
in the hilltop cemetery
a half mile north of our little town.

With that particular shovel
he cut the outline of the grave
to keep the lines straight,
not scooped. Even as a child
I recognized the beauty of straight lines,
the crisp edges where buffalo grass met
a hole in the ground.

On the evening before our father's funeral,
my brother, my husband, and I visited
the cemetery to see the plot
that had been prepared for Dad's eternal rest.

The grave had been excavated by a machine;
there were no clean edges. The walls were
not smooth and flat; they were gouged and uneven.
Tree roots extended into the open grave.
Although the roots were thin and would easily give
to the vault being lowered, they were unsightly;
my dad would've cut them away.

Our dark humor would've made Dad laugh.
He'd roll over in his grave
at seeing one so poorly dug—
but the truth remained:
our father deserved his perfect rectangle of space.

The East Row
of Junipers

After I pierced the earth with
a small bouquet of Memorial Day
flowers for my dad
and a small bouquet for Betty,
I sat, butt on the ground,
on Dad's grass-covered grave.

(I will add here that
the sitting-on-the-ground part of this scene
would *not* have happened if the
heart-rate-raising, nearly-stepping-on-a-snake
incident had happened two minutes *before*
I sat on the ground instead of two minutes
after rising from the earth.)

Songbirds offered a musical background
to the quiet setting, air barely moving,
buffalo grass still spring green, freshly mowed.

I took it all in—
the call of the meadowlark,
the gentle breeze, a swelling
of my heart with gratitude
for all that my father had given me,
including rich memories of this place.

Behind me, a row of juniper trees,
blue berries clustered among its needles.

When I was young,
my father planted this row of trees
along the eastern fence
and we hauled water from home
several times a week, Dad's pickup
full of deep buckets sloshing in the bed.
Dad poured water around the base
of each tree, a blessing absorbed by the soil.
Fifty years later, the trees are still doing
their job: defining the graveyard's boundary,
sheltering birds, offering shade.

You Can't Go Home Again

As I pass the city limits sign
driving into Pawnee Rock,
there's a pull, an energy
that captures me, and I want
to see everything, absorb everything,
store it all in my mind for future use.

A benefit of returning to Pawnee Rock
only about once a year now
is that I am able to keep
Past Pawnee Rock in a different part
of my brain from Present Pawnee Rock.

They are different towns.

The streets of my childhood town
were lined with fluffy green trees.
Elms in our yard dumped enough
autumn leaves to build a fort. Downtown
Pawnee Rock had cottonwoods in front
of the post office and Willard's Welding.
A dandy elm tree on the west side
of my dad's shop gave him afternoon shade.
But the best trees were two elms in front
of the lumberyard which, when climbed,
provided additional seating because
there was room for only three kids
on the lumberyard bench.

Every single one of those trees
is gone. Dutch elm disease hit in the '70s.
Time and storms took out more trees.
The town looks stripped, barren.

In the town of my childhood, my friends were
beside me walking to and from school,
playing hide and seek after dark with the boys,
riding bikes and the occasional horse.

My friends moved away. Relatives
have passed on to the next world.

Our house was simple but painted
every two years. And our yard was magical.
My parents created something
as close to a secret garden as
you'd find in the middle of Kansas.

Now, seeing my house and yard
just makes me sad. Many structures
in town have fallen into disrepair.
On each visit, there's more decay.

It feels like I don't belong there.
And I don't. I left,
so this isn't home anymore.

The Thread of Life

In my hometown cemetery,
I wandered among familiar names.
The older gravestones were ones
I had trimmed grass around
when I worked here with my dad
in the '60s and '70s.
I knew these old stones, these families,
by name only;
they had passed before I was born.

I smiled again to see
the black cylindrical stones
of John and Alice Daniels,
who died in 1904 and 1926.
These two stones were a favorite
when I was young. And as a kid,
I climbed the tree which stretched out
over the Logan family.
D. R. Logan died in 1924 at age 76.
He ran a successful general store during
Pawnee Rock's early days.

From among the granite stones
and the buffalo grass, I texted a few photos
to my brother.

Leon responded, mentioning the experience
that we gained by relying on hand clippers
instead of the weed-whackers used now:

"Imagine how different our childhoods
would've been if we hadn't
gotten to know the cemetery
clipping on our knees."

Yes. Hand-clipping the grass
at ground level is what connected me
to those who had their chance at life
before I had mine.

With each squeeze of the clippers,
with the brushing away of loose grass
from the base of the stone,
I contemplated the person buried there.
I did math to learn their age at death,
to discover the difference
in years between siblings.
Death is always about subtraction.

And yet, these dead people
whom I didn't know,
and the lives I imagined them to live,
added depth to my life,
added a way of moving time
both backward and forward.
I wanted somehow to continue
the thread of life that they started,
to live my life in honor of theirs.

Acknowledgments

I am deeply indebted to these fine folks:

My brother, my editor, Leon Unruh, for his enthusiastic and faithful dedication to the English language. He is the person I trust most with my words. Leon also designed the inside of this book. When I was a kid, Leon was my idol and he continues to be the best big brother a girl could ask for.

Tracy Million Simmons—my friend, writing buddy, critique group member, partner in *105 Meadowlark Reader* (a Kansas Journal of Creative Nonfiction), and, as the owner of Meadowlark Press, my publisher for this book—continually inspires me to be better, as a writer, as a human being.

Hazel Hart, friend and author of historical Kansas fiction, part of my three-person critique group, who has offered countless valuable suggestions over the years.

Emporia Writers Group. Since 2010, I have drunk coffee, tea, and beer with these writing friends. Meeting regularly with other writers has produced friendships and camaraderie, helpful feedback and unending support.

My Pawnee Rock friends and classmates who made my days there full of laughter and fun, especially Amy, Marilyn, Sarah, Jeanette, Darla, Karla, and Donna who all stay in touch and still fill my life with joy.

Pawnee Rock residents who watched out for me—the parents of my friends who were like second parents to me, and other members of the community who took an interest in the well-being of Pawnee Rock kids.

My dear mother, who has always encouraged my education and my writing and has been supportive of me since the beginning of time.

My late father, who inspired in me an appreciation of our hometown and our state.

My late stepmother, Betty. Find someone who loves you the way Betty loved my father.

My sweet husband and best friend, Dave, who can cook both a fantastic steak as well as delicious chicken biryani, and who cheers me on always, in all ways. Dave is responsible for the stunning cover photo and the author photo.

About the author

For 11 years Cheryl Unruh wrote a weekly newspaper column, "Flyover People," for William Allen White's newspaper, *The Emporia Gazette*. Her books of Kansas essays, *Flyover People* and *Waiting on the Sky*, published by Quincy Press, both received the Kansas Notable Book Award. Cheryl's collection of poetry, *Walking on Water*, was published by Meadowlark Press. She is the editor of *105 Meadowlark Reader*, a Kansas journal of creative nonfiction. Cheryl lives in Emporia, Kansas.

Meadowlark **MEMOIR**

Books are a way to explore, connect, and discover. Reading gives us the gift of living lives and gaining experiences beyond our own. Publishing books is our way of saying—

We love these words,
we want to play a role in preserving them,
and we want to help share them with the world.

Meadowlark Press
— since 2014 —

meadowlark-books.com

Made in the USA
Columbia, SC
02 December 2021